VIKING
SIDE HUSTLE

Chapter 1:

Intro to Side Hustles

Side hustles are a relatively new idea, with the term only being coined in the 1950s. A side hustle is a way people earn income outside of their regular jobs. The phrase has gained huge popularity in the past decade as more people are looking at ways to make a bit of extra cash. It's no coincidence that this popularity has paralleled a growth in the gig economy- with the advent of companies like Uber and AirBnB, many people can now bring in a second income without making huge adjustments to their lifestyle.

If you want to explore how you can make money in your spare time, this is the guide for you. Chapter one looks at the benefits you can get from side hustles, chapter two lays out some online side hustles you can do, and chapter three explores some offline side hustle options. By the time you've finished this book, you'll be able to find the perfect side hustle to match your schedule and needs.

According to research conducted by Princeton in 2017, over 44 million Americans have a side hustle going, covering almost every demographic of the population. Here's what the statistics have to say about who side hustles and why they do it:

- 86% of side hustlers do it at least once a month. This includes 96% of people between 18 and 26, and 83% of people over 26.
- The amount of money earned through side hustles tends to differ across generations.
- 36% of side hustlers earn more than $500 per month through their secondary work.
- 50% of baby boomers reach this income level, compared to just 19% of millennials, who on average, earn $200 per month.
- Those in their fifties and sixties are most likely to earn over $1,000 per month.
- Just over half of people who side hustle use the money they earn to cover necessary expenses, with only 46% seeing the money their side hustles earn as disposable income.
- How side hustle earnings are used varies according to gender, with women more than twice as likely as men to use their earnings to help with expenses.

The real question is, why do all these people have side hustles? The reasons range from pragmatic to personal, and it can be a good way to try something new if you're considering a career change, or just want a new hobby. As inflation rises and wages stay the same, side hustles give a lot of people comfort in the idea that they don't have to rely on traditional work models for all their income. The idea of work has changed a lot in recent decades, and the growing popularity of side hustles is giving more and more people the opportunity to mix work and play in a manner that works for them.

If you're considering a side hustle, your motivation could be financial, creative, or even just curiosity. Here are some great reasons to have a side hustle:

1.   Extra income.

There are so many reasons why you might want a second stream of income; paying off debts, building up savings, or even just so you can treat yourself every once in a while. Another great thing about a second source of income is that it means you aren't totally reliant on your day job. So many people are living paycheck to paycheck, which means that losing your job can mean losing everything else, too. A side hustle doesn't necessarily mean you'll make enough money to stop working, but it can give you a bit of extra financial security.

2.   You can indulge in your passion

Having a side hustle doesn't have to just be about making money, it can also be a chance for you to live that dream you never thought you could! A lot of people have very creative side hustles where they make art or sell things on Etsy, purely because they love the artistic process. It's just a happy bonus that they make some money doing it!

3.   You aren't taking a big risk

So many business owners talk about the big, scary leap they took when they decided to quit their job and build their business full-time. That kind of risk isn't feasible for everyone, and having a side hustle will allow you to work on your business without losing the security of your regular paycheck. This also means you'll be under less pressure to keep your business afloat if things aren't working out.

4.   You'll be more fulfilled

If you're considering starting a side hustle, examine your life right now and ask yourself what elements you are and aren't happy with. Would you like more financial stability? Would you like to be less stressed? Would you like to do something more productive than binge-watch Netflix every evening? Would you like to meet new people? Deciding what you want and curating your side hustle toward that will help you to have a better, happier lifestyle.

Chapter 2:

Online Side Hustle Ideas

The progression of internet and smartphone technology has allowed people to avail of new kinds of services, which in turn, create new kinds of jobs. The most popular forms of side hustle right now are all online, with people using websites and mobile apps to earn some extra income.

The benefits of online side hustles include being able to work from anywhere and getting started with nothing more than a laptop and internet connection. For these reasons, online side hustles are particularly popular with people who have hectic schedules, such as parents and shift workers. However, for some people, this instant access can sometimes be a negative. If you're the kind of person who feels like they already get enough work emails, having twice as much business communication might not be great for you.

Let's take a look at some of the most popular and lucrative online options when it comes to side hustles, and how each of them can be used to boost your finances.

Chapter 2:

Online Side Hustle Ideas

The progression of internet and smartphone technology has allowed people to avail of new kinds of services, which in turn, create new kinds of jobs. The most popular forms of side hustle right now are all online, with people using websites and mobile apps to earn some extra income.

The benefits of online side hustles include being able to work from anywhere and getting started with nothing more than a laptop and internet connection. For these reasons, online side hustles are particularly popular with people who have hectic schedules, such as parents and shift workers. However, for some people, this instant access can sometimes be a negative. If you're the kind of person who feels like they already get enough work emails, having twice as much business communication might not be great for you.

Let's take a look at some of the most popular and lucrative online options when it comes to side hustles, and how each of them can be used to boost your finances.

Teaching English

You've probably heard of people teaching English as a side hustle before, maybe even teaching English abroad while they travel. But did you know you can now do this work online? Online English lessons are incredibly popular across the world, so there's no shortage of work out there if you're interested. There are lots of companies you can work with as a native English speaker, but a good way to earn a higher hourly rate is do at TEFL course. TEFL (which stands for Teaching English as a Foreign Language) is an internationally-recognised system of teaching English, and TEFL-accredited teachers can earn great money online, as well as in physical classrooms. You can do a TEFL course online or in your local education centre.

Freelancing

"Freelancing" refers to working on contracts for a variety of clients, usually on an as-needed basis. This is a great option for creative people, and those who don't want to make a large time commitment to their side hustle. There are many freelance sites (such as Upwork and PeoplePerHour) where you can offer your services in different industries. Popular options for freelancers are programming, writing, and graphic design. If you don't have these specialist skills, there are also lots of jobs that can be done by anyone who has a good eye for detail, such as proofreading and being a virtual assistant.

Online surveys

Companies are always looking for feedback on their products, and there are lots of websites that reward you for filling out surveys about your customer experiences. This can be a great side hustle for some people, but there are a lot of survey sites that don't pay very well or pay in vouchers rather than cash. If you're looking for a side hustle to pay the bills, this isn't it. This is more suited to people who want to make a little extra cash without a lot of effort. Online surveys can be a nice way to earn some money while watching TV or waiting for the bus, but make sure you do your research and find a reliable site to work through.

Chapter 3:

Offline Side Hustle Ideas

If you aren't very tech-savvy or feel like you get enough screen time at your day job, there are lots of offline side hustles you can do that will put you in touch with the world around you.

Offline side hustles are a great way to get involved in your community, and can give you the opportunity to be more active and social. They can be limiting though, as you'll probably only work in your local area, and will need a car for a lot of jobs. However, if you like driving or want to use the opportunity to use your old bike again, an offline option could be the perfect fit for you!

A lot of offline side hustles can be done through the internet-this might seem like they're technically online, but usually the app or website is just used to help you find the work. Then, you can have all the real-world interactions your heart desires! Here are some of the most popular offline side hustle options:

Driving

If you have a car, registering for a ride sharing service can be a great way to make some extra money without having to do any specialist work. The two most popular services, Uber and Lyft, allow you to essentially become a freelance taxi driver. You work using a mobile app that tells you where to pick up and drop off customers, and you turn the app on and off depending on when you want to be available for work. Both services also have a "Destination Mode", in which you state where you're going and only pick up passengers that are going in the same direction. This can be a great way to make some money on your commute without too much of a detour.

Food delivery

Services like Seamless and GrubHub are always hiring drivers, and you can make $13 per hour plus tips if you take enough orders! All you need is a clean driver's licence and a phone to download their app. If you want to use your side hustle as an opportunity to get more exercise, these companies also hire cyclists!

Letting a room

If you have a spare bedroom, services like AirBnB and Homestay are a great way to make some money with a space that would otherwise just be unused. This can also be a great way to meet new people, particularly travellers from other countries, and maybe make some new friends! However, you need to be willing to open your home to strangers, so this is not a good option for those who enjoy their privacy. You can rent out a spare bedroom while you're at home, or rent out your entire property while you're on vacation or if you happen to have a second home. The options are flexible, and you can turn your availability on and off whenever you want. You can earn a good amount of money from this side hustle, especially if you make an effort to decorate the room and be a friendly host. This is a side hustle where you can be as involved or as passive as you like; it's all about what works for you.

The popularity of side hustles shows that there's a job out there to suit every type of lifestyle. Whether you have free evenings, a spare bedroom, or a secret artistic side, you'll be able to find a side hustle that adds to your life and brings in some money.

You can join over 44 million Americans who are side hustling, and potentially earn a few hundred dollars a month! You can work online using specialist skills, do menial tasks that don't take much energy, or work on a local level within your community, or even within your home. The world of side hustles is always growing, so go out there and explore until you find the perfect match for you.

www.ingramcontent.com/pod-product-compliance
Lightning Source LLC
Chambersburg PA
CBHW040932210326
41597CB00030B/5270